LATIN
FOR BEGINNERS

Angela Wilkes

Illustrated by John Shackell

Designed by Roger Priddy

Language consultants: Graham Tingay and Rubricastellanus
(Karl-Heinz Graf von Rothenburg)

Edited by Jane Chisholm

CONTENTS

2 About this book
4 Saying "Hello" and "Good-bye"
6 What is your name?
8 Naming things
10 Where do you come from?
12 More about you
14 Your family
16 Your home
18 Looking for things
20 What do you like to eat?
22 Table talk
24 Your hobbies

26 Telling time
28 Arranging things
30 Asking for directions
32 Finding your way around
34 Going shopping
36 Shopping and going to a café
38 Months and seasons
40 Colors and numbers
41 Pronunciation and grammar
42 More grammar
44 Vocabulary
46 Numbers, dates and time
47 Answers to puzzles

Latin was the language of the Ancient Romans. Although Romans nowadays speak Italian instead, Latin is still spoken in schools and universities all over the world. It is the official language of the Roman Catholic Church. Scientists use Latin for classifying and naming new species, and scholars even get together to agree on "new" Latin words for ordinary things, like *television* and *pizza*, that didn't exist in Roman times.

You can find out how to ...

talk about yourself,

and your home and family,

count and tell time,

ask for the food you like,

find your way around,

and go shopping.

How you learn

salve!

salve!

hic Petrus est.

The pictures show you what to say in each situation. Read the speech bubbles, and see how much you can understand by yourself. Then look up any words you do not know. Words and phrases are repeated again and again, to help you remember them. The book starts with things that are easy to say and gets harder as you go on.

New words

All the new words you come across are listed on each double page, so you can find them easily as you go along. If you forget a word, you can look it up in the Vocabulary on pages 44-45. If you see an asterisk* by a word, it means there is a note about it at the bottom of the page.

Grammar

Latin is easier if you know some of its grammar, or rules, but it doesn't matter if you don't understand it all right away. Boxes around words like the box below show where new grammar is explained. You can look up any of the grammar, including the rules about how Latin word endings change, on pages 41-43.

How to say things

Nobody knows exactly what Latin sounded like, so it is usually pronounced as it is written. There are accents on some of the words in the word lists in this book. You can find out how to use them on page 41.

Puzzles

All the way through the book there are puzzles and quizzes to help you practice your Latin and to test yourself on what you have learned. You can check whether your answers are right on pages 47-48.

Practicing your Latin

Write all the new words in a notebook, and try to learn a few every day. Keep going over them and you will soon remember them.

Ask a friend or someone in your family to test you. Better still, find someone to learn Latin with you, so you can test each other.

requiro . . .

Try to speak Latin whenever you can. Don't be afraid of making mistakes. Look out for Latin written on old buildings or churches.

Saying "Hello" and "Good-bye"

The first thing you should know how to say in Latin is "Hello." There are different greetings for different times of the day. Here you can find out what to say when.

salve/salvete**   hello
bonum diem   good day
bonam vésperum   good evening
bonam noctem   goodnight
vale/valete**   goodbye

It is polite to add **domine** (Sir) for a man, **domina** (Madam) for a woman, and **dominula** (Miss) for a girl.

Saying "Hello"

This is how you say "Hello" to a friend.

bonum diem means "Good day!"

This is how you say "Good evening."

Saying "Good-bye"

salve can mean "Good-bye" as well as "Hello."

vale means "Good-bye" and "Farewell."

Saying "Good-night"

You only use **bonam noctem** last thing at night.

How are you?

This means "How are you?"

This woman is saying that she is fine, thank you....

...but this man is saying that he isn't very well.

ut vales?

What do you think these people would say if you asked them how they were? Choose from the list below.

ut vales?	how are you?
bene váleo	I'm fine, well
grátias ago	thank you
óptime	very well
bene	well
satis bene	quite well
non ita bene	not very well
péssime	terrible

What is your name ?

Here you can find out how to ask someone their name and tell them yours, and how to introduce your friends. Read the picture strip and see how much you can understand. Then try doing the puzzles on the opposite page.

New words

quod nomen tibi est ?	what's your name?
mihi nomen est	my name is
quod est nomen amícae meae?	what is my friend's name?
nomen meum	my name
nomen tuum	your name
nomen eius	his/her name
nómina eorum	their names
amícus meus est	he is my friend
amíca mea	my (girl) friend
quis?	who?
hic puer	this boy
haec puélla	this girl
et tibi?	and you?
quis est hic /haec*?	who is this (boy/girl)?
quod ... est?	what is...?
quae ... sunt?	what are...?
ita est!	so it is / yes
non	not
sed	but
sunt	(they) are

Questions

Questions in Latin sometimes have a questioning word at the beginning, such as **quis** (who?), **cur** (why?), **quando** (when?), or **ut** (how?). If there is no questioning word, **-ne** is added to the end of the first word. This shows that the sentence is a question. For example, **"estne nomen eius Petrus?"** means "Is his name Peter?".

Introducing friends

6   * To find out more about **hic** and **haec**, see page 8.

What are their names?

Can you answer these questions in Latin?

quod est nomen amicae meae?

quod nomen tibi est?

quod nomen eius est?

quae nomina eorum sunt?

Who is who?

Can you answer the questions below the picture?

salve, ut vales?

bene valeo, gratias ago.

vale, Carole.

estne haec puella Cornelia?

ita est! nomen eius Cornelia est.

vale.

quis est hic puer?

nomen eius Quintus est.

mihi nomen Marcus non est, sed Lucius.

estne tibi nomen Marcus?

quod nomen tibi est?

Beata, et tibi?

Who is talking to Quintus?	Which person is Lucius?	Who is reading the paper?
Who is talking to Beata?	Who is speaking to him?	Who is going home?

Can you remember?

How would you ask someone's name?
How would you tell them your name?

You have a friend named Beata.
How would you introduce her?
How would you tell someone that your friend's name is Gaius?

7

Finding out what things are called

Everything in this picture has its name on it. See if you can learn the names for everything. Then try the quiz in the box at the bottom of the opposite page.

caminus(m)

tectum(n)

sol(m)

avis(f)

salvete!

nidus(m)

arbor(f)

fenestra(f)

flos(f)

domus(f)

haec domus mea est.

porta(f)

stabulum autocineticum(n)

saeptum(n)

feles(f)

canis(m)

autocinetum(n)

Nouns

All Latin nouns are either masculine, feminine, or neuter (neither). This is called their gender. The gender is shown in the vocabulary by the letters **m**, **f** and **n**. Many masculine nouns end in **-us**, feminine nouns in **-a** and neuter nouns in **-um**. But there are many exceptions and many other endings too. Men are masculine and women are feminine, but there is no way of guessing the gender of most things. You just have to learn

them. The endings of words also change according to how they are used. The different endings, called cases, will be explained later.

There is no word in Latin for "the" or "a," but you can often use the word "this" instead. The word for this is **hic** (**m**), **haec** (**f**), **hoc** (**n**). The one you choose depends on the gender of the noun. For example, **hic nidus** (**m**). **hic** and **haec** can sometimes be used to mean "he" and "she."

New words

étiam	also
arbor (f)	tree
domus (f)	house
cáminus (m)	chimney
avis (f)	bird
tectum (n)	roof
Latíne/Anglice	in Latin/ English
fenéstra (f)	window
flos (f)	flower
porta (f)	door
canis (m)	dog
feles (f)	cat
nidus (m)	nest
sol (m)	sun
autocinéticum (n)	car
stábulum autocinéticum (n)	
	garage
saeptum (n)	fence

quid hoc est?

hic flos est.

etiamne flos est?

non flos sed arbor est?

quid est hoc Latine?

haec est porta.

et quid hoc est?

hic canis est.

quid est hoc Anglice?

A dog.

Can you remember?

Cover up the word lists, and see if you can name these things in Latin. Begin your answers with **hic est**, **haec est** or **hoc est**.

9

Where do you come from?

Here you can find out how to ask people where they come from. You can also find out if they can speak Latin.

New Words

unde venis?	where do you come from?
vénio e/ex	I come from...
ubi hábitas?	where do you live?
hábito (in)	I live in...
loquor	I speak
scio	I know (how to)
scisne loqui...?	can you speak...?
paulum	a little
Latíne	(in) Latin
Gállice	(in) French
Germánice	(in) German
Ánglice	(in) English
ecce	here is...
et	and
-que (on the end of a word)	and
Lóndinii	in London
Lutétiae	in Paris
Gállia	France
Caledónia	Scotland
Hispánia	Spain
Germánia	Germany
Itália	Italy
Hungária	Hungary

Where do you come from?

unde venis?

e Britannia venio.

ubi habitas?

Londinii habito.

unde venis?

e Germania venio.

amica mea e Gallia venit, et Lutetiae habitat.

Can you speak Latin?

scisne loqui Latine?

Latine paulum loqui scio.

scisne loqui Latine, Octavia?

loquor Latine et paulum Anglice.

Henricus scit loqui Latine et Anglice et Germanice.

Who comes from where?

These are the contestants for an international dance competition. They have come from all over the world. The organizer cannot speak any Latin and does not understand where anyone comes from. Read about the contestants. Then see if you can tell him what he wants to know. His questions are beneath the picture.

Angus
e Caledonia
venit.

ecce Maria
et Petrus!
e Gallia
veniunt.

Arius et Indira
ex India veniunt.

Ianus ex
Hungaria venit.
habitat
Aquinci.

Franciscus ex
Austria venit.

ecce Lolita!
ex Hispania
venit.

Where do
they all
come from?

Where does Franz (Franciscus) come from?
What are the names of the Indians?
Is Lolita Italian or Spanish?
Who lives in Budapest (Aquincum)?

Is there a Scottish contestant?
Where do Marie and Pierre (Maria and Petrus) come from?
Where is Budapest?

Verbs (action words)

Latin verbs change their endings according to who is doing the action. Verbs ending in **-are** follow the same pattern as **habitare**. Verbs ending in **-ire** (such as **scire**) are like **venire**.

habitare	to live in	venire	to come
habit-o*	I live in	**veni-o**	I come
habit-as	you live in	**veni-s**	you come
habit-at	he/she lives in	**veni-t**	he/she comes
habit-amus	we live in	**veni-mus**	we come
habit-atis	you live in	**veni-tis**	you come
habit-ant	they live in	**veni-unt**	they come

Can you remember?

How would you ask someone where they come from?
How do you say that you can speak Latin?

Can you say where you come from?
How do you ask someone else if they can speak Latin?

*In Latin, you do not need a separate word for "I," "you," "we," etc. There is more about verbs on pages 41 and 42.　11

More about you

Here you can find out how to say how old you are, how many brothers and sisters you have, and how to count up to 20.

In Latin, a boy says **decem annos natus sum** for "I am ten years old," and a girl says **decem annos nata sum.**

New words

quot?	how many?
quot annos?	how many years?
natus, -a, -um	born
tu	you (singular)
mihi est/sunt...	I have...
tibi est/sunt...	you have...
frater meus	my brother
fratres	brothers
soror mea	my sister
soróres	sisters
paene	almost, nearly
neque...neque	neither...nor

Describing words

The endings of Latin adjectives change according to the word they describe. For example, in the singular you use **natus** for masculine words, **nata** for feminine words and **natum** for neuter words. In the plural, the masculine is **nati**, the feminine is **natae** and the neuter is **nata.**

Numbers*

1 unus, una, unum
2 duo, duae, duo
3 tres, tres, tria
4 quáttuor
5 quinque
6 sex
7 septem
8 octo
9 novem
10 decem

How old are you?

Do you have any brothers or sisters?

12 *There is a longer list of numbers on page 40.

How old are they?

Read what these children are saying. Then see if you can say how old they are.

- Titus duodecim annos natus est.
- quindecim annos natae sumus.
- Livia undecim annos nata est.
- Marcus paene quattuordecim annos natus est.
- quinque annos nata sum, hic novem annos natus est.

Marcus   Diana et Sylvia   Titus   Livia   Lucius   Aemilia

Brothers and sisters

Below you can read how many brothers and sisters the children have. Can you figure out who has which brothers and sisters?

Dianae et Sylviae unus frater et duo sorores sunt.

Liviae tres sorores et duo fratres sunt.

Marco quinque sorores, sed fratres non sunt.

Lucio unus frater est, sed sorores non sunt.

Tito neque fratres neque sorores sunt, sed canis ei est.

The verb "to be"

esse	to be
sum	I am
es	you are
est	he/she/it is
sumus	we are
estis	you are (plural)
sunt	they are

The dative

mihi	to me
tibi	to you
ei	to him
Lucio	to Lucius

The Latin for "Titus has one brother" is **est Tito unus frater**, which literally means "To Titus is one brother." This uses the dative case, shown here.

Talking about your family

You will find lots of words on these two pages to help you talk about your family.

Many of the phrases include the words "my" and "your."

ecce familia mea.

canis meus

meus avus

meus pater

soror mea

patruus meus

feles mea

avia mea

mater mea

frater meus

amita mea

Who's who?

estne hic frater tuus?

ita est. frater meus est.

estne haec soror tua?

ita est. nomen eius Licinia est.

suntne hi parentes tui?

minime! avus et avia sunt.

New words

família (f)	family	**ego**	I	**parvus, -a, -um**	little
paréntes (m)	parents	**nos**	we	**crassus, -a, -um**	fat
pater (m)	father	**avúnculus (m)**	uncle	**grácilis, -is, -e**	thin
mater (f)	mother	**pátruus (m)**	uncle	**flavus, -a, -um**	blond, yellow
avus (m)	grandfather	**ámita (f)**	aunt	**fuscus, -a, -um**	dark
ávia (f)	grandmother	**matértera (f)**	aunt	**tener, -era, -erum**	gentle
		magnus, -a, -um	large	**vetérrimus, -a, -um**	very old

"My" and "your"

The words for "my" and "your" vary, just like other adjectives. They have to agree with the gender and number of the noun (whether it is singular or plural).

	masculine	feminine	neuter
my (singular)	**meus**	**mea**	**meum**
your (singular)	**tuus**	**tua**	**tuum**
my (plural)	**mei**	**meae**	**mea**
your (plural)	**tui**	**tuae**	**tua**

14

Describing your family

pater meus magnus,
sed mater mea
parva est.

mater mea magna,
sed pater
meus parvus est.

patruus meus crassus,
sed amita mea
gracilis est.

avus meus
veterrimus est.
ego parvus sum.

soror mea
flava est.
frater meus
fuscus est.

canis meus
tener est.

Describing words

As you learned on page 12, Latin adjectives* change their endings according to the gender of the word they are describing. Many end in **-us**, **-a**, **-um**. Some others end in **-is**, **-is**, **-e** in the singular, and **-es**, **-es**, **-ia** in the plural.

Can you describe each of these people in Latin, using the new words you have learned?

Start with **hic** or **haec est**...

* You can find out more about adjectives on page 43.

Your home

Here you can find out how to say what sort of home you live in, and where it is. You can also learn what all the rooms are called.

New words

aut	or
domus (f)	house
ínsula (f)	apartment
palátium (n)	palace
in urbe	in the city
ruri	in the country
ad mare	at, by the sea
papa (m)	Dad
mamma (f)	Mom
larva (f)	ghost
ubi es/estis?	where are you?
bálneum (n)	bathroom
cenáculum (n)	dining room
cubículum (n)	bedroom
mediánum (n)	living room
coquína (f)	kitchen
vestíbulum (n)	hall
tabulátum (n)	story, floor
in summo tabuláto	on the top floor
hábito	I live in

Where do you live?

habitasne in domo aut insula?

in domo habito.

in insula habito.

in palatio habito.

City or country?

in urbe habito.

ruri habito.

ad mare habito.

Where is everyone?

Dad comes home and wants to find out where everyone is. Look at the pictures and see if you can tell him. (For example, **avia in mediano est.**)

Then see if you can answer the questions below the little pictures.

mater   pater   avus

avia   Petrus   Isabella

Quintus   larva

quis in cenaculo est?
quis in coquina est?
quis in balneo est?
quis in cubiculo est?

ubi avia est?
ubi larva est?
ubi Isabella est?
ubi Petrus est?

in summo tabulato sum.

in cubiculo Isabellae sum.

in balneo sum.

in mediano sum.

in cubiculo sum.

ubi estis?

in cenaculo sum.

in coquina sum.

Can you remember?

Cover up the pictures and see if you can remember how to say these things. The answers are on page 47.

I live in a city. You live in the country.
The bedroom is on the top story.

Grandma lives in an apartment building.
Quintus is in the bathroom.
We live in a house.

Looking for things

Here you can find out how to ask someone what they are looking for and tell them where things are. You can also learn lots of words for things around the house.

New words

quaero	I look for
quaeris	you look for
áliquid	something
cricétus (m)	a hamster
repério	I find
eum/eam/id	him/her/it
in armário	in/on the cupboard
sub sponda	under the sofa
post velum	behind the curtain
inter plantas	among the plants
sponda (f)	sofa
sella (f)	chair
velum (n)	curtain
planta (f)	plant
mensa (f)	table
librárium (n)	bookcase
tapéte (n)	carpet
televisórium (n)	television
telephónum (n)	telephone
vásculum (n)	vase

Prepositions

ad	at, to, by the side of (+ acc.)
ab	by, from (+ abl.)
ante	in front of (+ acc.)
e, ex	out of (+ abl.)
in	in (+ abl.), into (+ acc.)
post	behind, after (+ acc.)
prope	near (+ acc.)
sub	under (+ acc. & abl.)

The accusative case* for nouns ending in -us or -um is -um, and the ablative case is -o. For nouns ending in -a, the accusative is -am and the ablative is -a.

The missing hamster

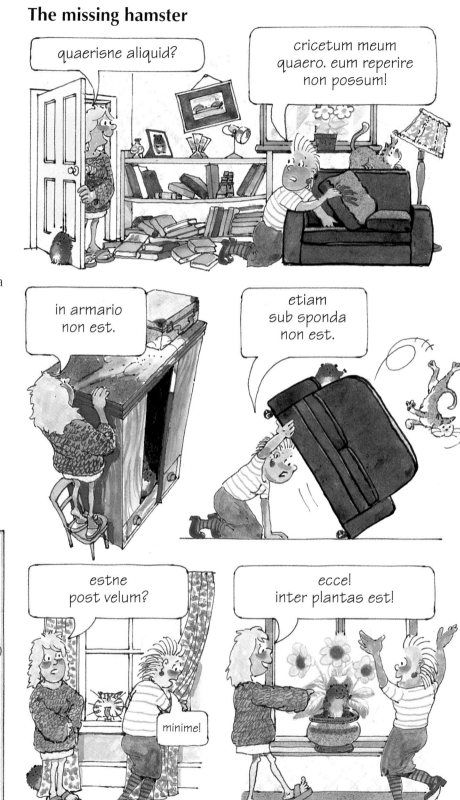

quaerisne aliquid?

cricetum meum quaero. eum reperire non possum!

in armario non est.

etiam sub sponda non est.

estne post velum?

minime!

ecce! inter plantas est!

*You can find out more about cases on page 42.

In, on or under?

in cista means "in the box." What do the other phrases mean? See how the ending of **cista** changes with the different prepositions.

in cista

post cistam

ante cistam

ad cistam

sub cista   in cista

Where are the animals hiding?

Grandfather's six pets are hiding somewhere in the room. Can you tell him where they are, using the prepositions above and giving each noun the right ending?

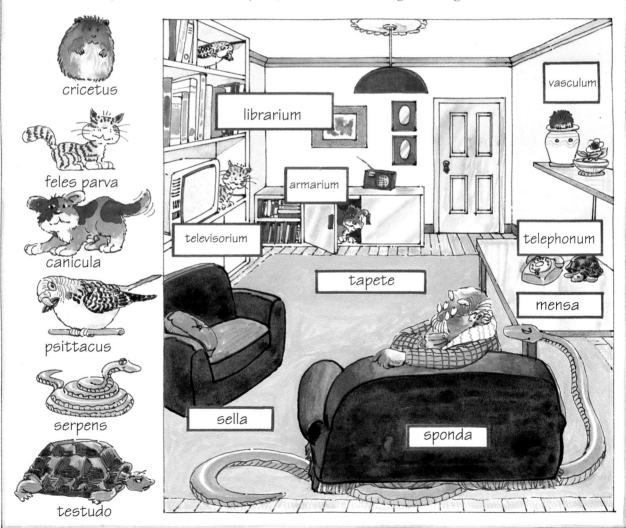

cricetus

feles parva

canicula

psittacus

serpens

testudo

vasculum

librarium

armarium

televisorium

tapete

telephonum

mensa

sella

sponda

What do you like to eat?

Here you can learn lots of food words and find out how to say what you like and don't like.

New words

amare	to like, love
amo	I like
amas	you like
amat	he/she likes
quid?	what?
quid ergo?	what then?
valde	very much
mínime	not at all
tum	then
máxime	most, best
praéfero	I prefer
edo	I eat
ego quoque	I also
láctuca (f)	lettuce
piscis (m)	fish
poma terréstria assa (n.pl)	french fries
placénta (f)	cake
bótulus (m)	sausage
búbula assa (f)	steak
pasta vermiculáta (f)	spaghetti
pitta (f)	pizza
Hammaburgénsis (m)	hamburger
óryza (f)	rice
panis (m)	bread
cáseus (m)	cheese
scriblíta (f)	a tart

What would you like?

amasne lactucam?

lactucam non amo.

amasne piscem?

minime!

quid ergo amas?

amo poma terrestria assa.

valde placentam amo.

What do you like most ?

quid maxime amas?

valde botulum amo.

sed bubulam assam praefero...

pastam vermiculatam amo.

What are they eating?

quid edis?

pittam edo.

poma terrestria assa edit.

panem et caseum edit.

Hammaburgenses edimus.

oryzam editis.

bananas edunt.

Who likes what?

Who likes cheese? Who likes ham?
Who prefers grapes to bananas?

Can you say in Latin which things you like
and which you don't like?

ego quoque,
sed pernam non amo.

bananas amo.

sed ego uvas praefero.

Marcus

caseum amo.

Julius

avus

maxime amo scriblitam pomorum.

Henricus

Julia

perna

butyrum

scriblita casei

panis

lactuca

caseus

bananae

uvae

tomatae

scriblita pomorum

aranciata

Subject and object

In the sentence **avus pernam amat**
("Grandfather likes ham."), **avus** is the
subject and **pernam** is the object. In Latin,
the subject uses the nominative case.*

The object uses the accusative case. This is why
when Henricus says **caseum amo** ("I love
cheese"), **caseum** is in the accusative.

*You can find more about different cases on pages 42-43.

21

Table talk

Here you can learn about things to say during a meal.

New words

veníte ad mensam!	come to the table!
quaeso	I beg/please
esúrio	I am hungry
sume áliquid!	Take something!
bene tibi sápiat!	Bon appetit!
sapítne bene?	Does it taste good?
óptime	excellent
potésne mihi dare...	Can you give me...
aqua/aquam (acc.) (f)	water
panis/panem (acc.) (m)	bread
hýalus/hýalum (acc.) (m)	a glass
caro/carnem (acc.) (f)	meat
visne áliquid?	Would you like something?
volo	I wish, want
vis	you wish, want
etiam	also
nolo	I don't want
satis	enough
estne bonum?	Is it good?
óptimum est!	It's very good!

Dinner is ready

venite ad mensam!

esurio.

ego quoque.

sume aliquid, quaeso!

gratias ago.

bene tibi sapiat!

bene tibi sapiat!

Please will you pass me...

da mihi aquam, quaeso.

da mihi panem, quaeso.

da mihi hyalum, quaeso.

Would you like some more?

visne etiam carnem?

volo!

visne etiam poma terrestria assa?

nolo. satis est.

sapitne bene?

optime sapit!

Who is saying what?

These little pictures show different mealtime situations. Cover up the rest of the page and see if you know what each of them would say in Latin.

Julius is crying that he is hungry.	The chef wants you to enjoy your meal.	Julia is saying "Help yourself."	Peter wants someone to give him a glass.
Julius's mother asks him if he wants more french fries.	He says "Yes, please," and that he likes french fries.	Then he says "No thanks," he's had enough.	Mark is saying the food tastes delicious.

Nouns and cases

Here are the endings of most of the nouns and cases you have met so far. Another group of nouns ends in **-em** in the accusative singular, and **-es** in the accusative plural.

Singular				Plural			
Nom.	**-us**	**-a**	**-um**	Nom.	**-i**	**-ae**	**-a**
Acc.	**-um**	**-am**	**-um**	Acc.	**-os**	**-as**	**-a**
Dat.	**-o**	**-ae**	**-o**	Dat.	**-is**	**-is**	**-is**

23

Your hobbies

These people are talking about their hobbies.

New words

píngere	to paint
cóquere	to cook
mihi placet...	I like to...
plassáre	to make models
saltáre	to dance
légere	to read
spectáre	to watch/look at
téxere	to weave/knit
natáre	to swim
audíre	to listen to
athlética (f)	sport
cánere	to play (an instrument)
lúdere	to play (a game)
pedifóllis (m)	football
tenilúdium (n)	tennis
música (n.pl)	music
instruméntum músicum (n)	musical instrument
violína (f)	violin
claviárium (n)	piano
vésperi	in the evening
sóleo...	I usually
libri (m. pl)	books

More verbs

Two different types of verb endings were shown on page 11. Here are two more.

placere*	to please
plac-eo	I please
plac-es	you please
plac-et	he/she/it pleases
plac-emus	we please
plac-etis	you please
plac-ent	they please

ludere*	to play
lud-o	I play
lud-is	you play
lud-it	he/she/it plays
lud-imus	we play
lud-itis	you play
lud-unt	they play

> quid tibi facere placet?

> pingere mihi placet.

> sed coquere mihi non placet.

> quid ergo tibi placet?

> mihi placet plassare.

> mihi placet saltare.

What do you do in the evenings?

> quid vesperi facis?

> aut libros legere...

> ...aut televisorium spectare et texere soleo.

*placere rhymes with "airy." ludere rhymes with "prudery."

The sporty type

quid tibi placet?

athletica mihi placet.

mihi natare placet.

ego pedifolle ludo.

et ego teniludio ludo.

Music lovers

quid vobis placet?

nobis musica audire placet.

canitisne instrumentis musicis?

clavario cano.

ita est. violina cano.

What are they doing?

A   B   C   E   D

Can you say in Latin what these people are doing? (E.g. A: **hic coquit**.) How would you ask the cook what he is doing? What would he answer? And the others?

Telling time

Here you can find out how to tell and ask for the time in Latin. For "one o'clock" in Latin, you would say **prima hora** (first hour).

The Ancient Romans divided the day in a different way from us. You can find out how they told time on page 46.

New words

dic mihi	tell me
quota hora est?	What time is it?
prima hora est.	It's one o'clock.
secúnda hora est.	It's two o'clock
quinque minútae ante/post +acc.	five minutes to/after…
quadrans ante/ post + acc.	a quarter to../ after…
quadránte...	at a quarter…
tértia hora et dimídia	half past three
merídies (m)	noon
média nox (f)	midnight
mane (n)	(in the) morning
súrgere	to get up
ientáculum (n)	breakfast
prándium (n)	lunch
cena (f)	dinner, supper
in scholam ire	to go to school
dórmitum ire	to go to bed

First, second, third...

1st	**primus,**	-a,	-um
2nd	**secúndus,**	-a,	-um
3rd	**tértius,**	-a,	-um
4th	**quartus,**	-a,	-um
5th	**quintus,**	-a,	-um
6th	**sextus,**	-a,	-um
7th	**séptimus,**	-a,	-um
8th	**octávus,**	-a,	-um
9th	**nonus,**	-a,	-um
10th	**décimus,**	-a,	-um
11th	**úndecimus,**	-a,	-um
12th	**dúodecimus,**	-a,	-um

What time is it?

This is how you ask for the time.

The time is...

quinque minutae sunt post nonam horam.

quadrans post nonam horam est.

nona hora est et dimidia.

quadrans ante decimam (horam)

quinque minutae ante decimam

meredies/media nox

What time of day?

sexta hora ante meridiem est.

sexta hora post meridiem est.

26

Marcus's day

Read what Marcus does during the day. Then see if you can match each clock with the right picture. You can check your answers on page 48.

A   B   C   D   E   F   G   H

1 — Marcus surgit septima hora et dimidia.

2 — hora octava ientaculum sumit.

3 — quadrante ante novam in scholam it.

4 — duodecima et dimidia prandium sumit.

5 — decem minutis post secundam pedifolle ludit.

6 — quadrante post quintam televisorium spectat.

7 — sexta hora cenam sumit.

8 — octava hora et dimidia dormitum it.

What time is it?

Can you say in Latin what times these clocks show?

27

Arranging things

Here is how to arrange to do things with your friends.

New words

quando	when
usque ad + acc.	until...
post merídiem	in the afternoon
bene	good
hódie	today
vésperi	in the evening
cras (adverb)	tomorrow
dies crastínus (m)	tomorrow
possum	I can
potes	you can
adíre cínema	to go to the movies
ádibis	you will go to
ludémus	we will play
natábimus	we will swim
convívium (n)	party
discothéca (f)	disco
saltáre	to dance
dóleo quod	I am sorry that

Days of the week

dies Lunae	Monday
dies Martis	Tuesday
dies Mercúrii	Wednesday
dies Iovis	Thursday
dies Véneris	Friday
dies Satúrni	Saturday
dies Solis	Sunday

Tennis

Swimming

Going to the movies

28

Going to a party

Your diary for the week

This is your diary for the week. Read it and see if you can answer the questions.

What are you doing on Friday evening?
When are you playing tennis?
What are you doing on Tuesday afternoon?

dies Lunae
4.hora   teniludium

dies Martis
2.hora   clavarium
5.30   natare

dies Mercurii
3.hora   teniludium
7.45   cinema

dies Iovis

dies Veneris
8.hora   saltare cum Tito

dies Saturni
2.hora   pediludium
7.hora   convivium

dies Solis
post meridiem:
teniludium

The ablative

The ablative is one of the six cases used with Latin nouns. It is used for time. For example **die** (abl.) **Lunae** means "on Monday." It is also used with prepositions. **in urbe** (abl.) means "in the city."

The future

	I will...	you	he/she/it
habitare (to live):	**habitabo,**	-abis,	-abit*
placere (to please):	**placebo,**	-ebis,	-ebit
ludere (to play):	**ludam,**	-es,	-et
venire (to come):	**veniam,**	-ies,	-iet

*You can find the future tense conjugated in full on page 42.

Asking for directions

The next three pages show you how to find your way around.

New Words

da mihi véniam	excuse me
illic, ibi	there
nihil labóris est	it's no trouble
in diréctum	straight ahead
flecte te	turn (to the)
sinistrórsum	left
dextrórsum	(to the) right
deinde	then
a laeva parte	on the left
a dextra parte	on the right
officium	
postále (n)	post office
deversórium	
statiónis	railroad
ferriviáriae (n)	station hotel
ubi est?	where is?
forum (n)	market place
in propínquo	nearby
i, ibis	go!, you
	will go
estne longínquum?	is it far?
fere	almost
minúta (f)	a minute
pédibus	on foot,
	walking
cafea (f)	café, coffee
pharmacopóla (f)	pharmacy
argentária (f)	bank
contra	against,
	across from
supermercátus (m)	supermarket

Being polite

> da mihi veniam, domine...

> gratias ago.

> nihil laboris est.

To ask something politely, remember to add **domine**, **domina** or **dominula**.

If someone thanks you for something, it is polite to answer **nihil laboris est**.

Where is...?

> da mihi veniam domina, ubi est officium postale?

> illic, in foro.

> ubi est, quaeso, deversorium stationis ferriviariae?

> flecte te sinistrorsum, deinde i in directum.

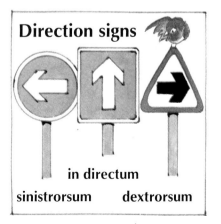

Direction signs

in directum

sinistrorsum   dextrorsum

Is there a . . . nearby?

Is it far?

Other useful places to ask for

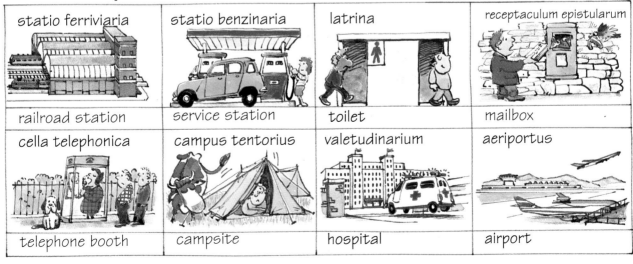

statio ferriviaria	statio benzinaria	latrina	receptaculum epistularum
railroad station	service station	toilet	mailbox
cella telephonica	campus tentorius	valetudinarium	aeriportus
telephone booth	campsite	hospital	airport

Finding your way around

Here you can find out how to ask your way around and follow directions. When you have read everything else, try the map puzzle on the opposite page.

da mihi veniam, qua via ad stationem ferriviariam venio?

flecte te dextrorsum, deinde i secunda via sinistrorsum.

statio ferriviaria a dextra parte sita est.

qua via ad deverticulum iuvenum venio?

i in directum usque ad ferriviariam stationem...

. . . deinde cape tertiam viam a dextra.

qua via ad praefecturam commeatus venio?

autoraedane? vehere in directum...

. . . deinde cape proximam viam a sinistra.

New words

qua via vénio ad..?	how do I get to…?	**praefectúra commeátus (f)**	tourist office
cape	take	**cúria (f)**	city hall
véhere	drive!	**tabérna (f)**	shop, store
autoraedáne?	by car?	**piscína (f)**	swimming pool
via prima	first street	**deversórium (n)**	hotel
via próxima	next street	**ecclésia (f)**	church
devertículum júvenum (n)	youth hostel	**sita est**	is situated

The imperative form

The imperative is the part of the verb you use for giving orders. Here are some examples in the singular: **i** (go!), **veni** (come!), **flecte** (turn!), **cape** (take!), **vehere** (drive!) and **da** (give!). There is more about the imperative on page 41.

Finding your way around Messina

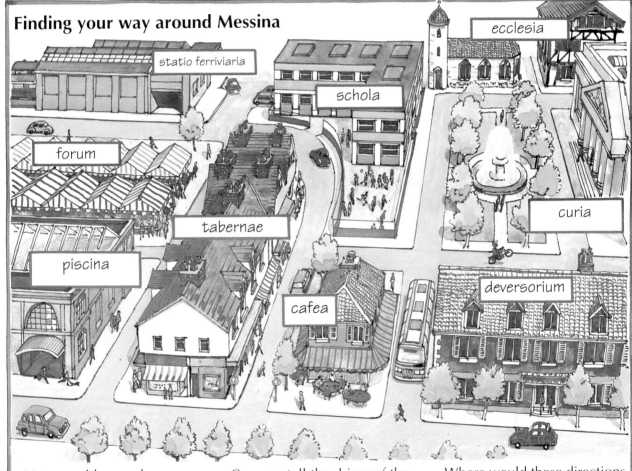

How would you ask someone the way to the market place? How would you ask if there is a café nearby?

Can you tell the driver of the red car how to get to the railroad station? Then tell the driver of the yellow car how to get to the church.

Where would these directions take the yellow car?
i secunda via sinistrorsum, deinde vehere semper in directum.

33

Going shopping

Here you can find out what to say in Latin when you go shopping.

New words

émere	to buy
cibária (n.pl)	food
pistrína (f)	bakery
tabérna	
alimentária (f)	grocery store
laniéna (f)	butcher shop
lac (n)	milk
ovum (n)	egg
pomum (n)	fruit
hólera (n.pl)	vegetables
caro (f)	meat
panicéllus (m)	roll, bun
malum (m)	apple
tomáta (f)	tomato
quid requíris?	what do you want?
pecúnia (f)	money
quid áliud?	what else?
quanti constant?	how much do they cost?
ómnia	everything
nihil iam	nothing now
libra (f)	pound (weight)

Roman money

Throughout the long history of the Roman empire, the look and value of coins was always changing, just as they do today. The coins in use were:

quadrans (copper)
semis (copper) = **2 quadrántes**
as (copper) = **2 semísses**
dupóndius (copper) = **2 asses**
sestértius (copper) = **2 dupóndii**
denárius (silver) = **4 sestértii**
aúreus (gold) = **25 denárii**

Although it was not worth very much, the **sestertius** was the coin the Romans used most often when describing the value of something. It was rather like a U.S. cent or a British Penny.

Cornelia goes shopping

Cornelia cibaria emit.

PISTRINA

in pistrina panem emit.

In the bakery

*The abbreviation for **sestertii** was HS. 50 **sestertii** was written HS L. You can find out how the Romans wrote their numbers on page 46.

lac et ova in taberna
alimentaria emit.

poma et holera in foro
emit.

carnem in laniena emit.

At the grocery store

quid requiris?

requiro sex ova, quaeso.

quid aliud?

unam litram lactis, quaeso.

quanti constant haec omnia?

omnia constant centum viginti sestertiis.

HSCXX

At the market

salve, domina! quid requiris?

requiro duas libras malorum.

quid aliud?

unam libram tomatarum.

haec omnia octoginta* sestertiis.

HS LXXX

*You will find a list of Latin numbers on page 40.

Shopping and going to a café

Here you can find out how to ask how much things cost and how to order in a café.

New words

chártula (f) postcard
rosa (f) rose
rátio/ratiónem (acc.f) check
aráncium (n) orange
aranciáta (f) orange juice
ananása (f) pineapple
cítreum (n) lemon
limonáta (f) lemonade
pérsicum (n) peach
cola (f) cola
thea (f) tea
cum lacte with milk
cum citreo with lemon
potus socolatae (m) chocolate drink
glácies (f) ice cream
velim I would like
hyalus (m) a glass
cafea (f) a café, coffee
quanti constat...? how much does...cost?
quanti constant...? how much do...cost?

Asking how much things cost

quanti constat haec chartula?

quindecim sestertiis.

quanti constant, quaeso, uvae?

una libra constat nonaginta sestertiis.

HSXC

quanti constant rosae?

una rosa constat sexaginta sestertiis.

da mihi, quaeso, septem rosas.

HS LX

Going to a café

quid requiris, quaeso?

velim cafeam.

ecce!

gratias ago!

rationem velim.

constat septuaginta sestertiis.

36

Buying fruit

Everything on the fruit stand is marked with its name and price. Look at the picture and see if you can answer the questions below it.

How do you tell the vendor you would like four lemons, a pound of bananas and a pineapple? How much do each of these things cost? How much is the total?

quid constat HS CX?
quid constat HS CCLX?
quanti constant tres aranciae?
quanti constat una libra malorum?

In the café

Here are some things you might order in a café.

velim...

unam limonatam	unam colam	unam theam cum lacte	unam theam cum citreo
unam aranciatam	unum potum socolatae	unum hyalum lactis	unam glaciem

Months, seasons and dates

Here you can learn what the seasons and months are called and find out how to say what the date is.

New Words

annus, anni (gen. m) year
mensis, -sis (gen. m) month
natális (m) birthday
hódie today
qui dies? what day?
quando? when?

The seasons

ver (n) spring
aestas (f) summer
autúmnus (m) autumn
hiems (f) winter

The months

Ianuárius, -arii January
Februárius, -arii February
Mártius, -tii March
Aprílis, -is April
Maius, -ii May
Iúnius, -ii June
Iúlius, -ii July
Augústus, -i August
Septémber, -bris September
Octóber, -bris October
Novémber, -bris November
Decémber, -bris December

The seasons

ver

Martius, Aprilis, Maius

aestas

Iunius, Iulius, Augustus

autumnus

September, October, November

hiems

December, Ianuarius, Februarius...

The genitive and ablative

The genitive case is used for "of..": e.g. **anni** (of the year). The ablative case is used for time and often means "on" or "at": e.g. **secundo die Maii** (on the second day of May). It is also used (often with prepositions) to mean "by," "with" or "from": e.g., **cum meo patre** (with my father) and **ex urbe** (from the city). Another use is for describing a position: e.g. **a sinistra parte** (on the left) and **in urbe** (in the city).

Ianuarius primus mensis anni est.

Februarius secundus mensis anni est.

December duodecimus mensis anni est.

Can you decribe the other months of the year in the same way?

What is the date?*

hodie tertius dies Maii est.

qui dies hodie est?

hodie primus dies Ianuarii est.

Writing the date

Romae, die 3.° mensis Maii.

The little sign ° is the abbreviation of the ordinal number (first, second, third..). For example, 2.° is **secundo** (second).

When is your birthday?

quando tuus natalis est?

die 10.° mensis Novembris.

natalis meus est die 12.° mensis Februarii.

natalis Iulii est die 8.° mensis Iunii.

When are their birthdays?

The dates of the children's birthdays are written below their pictures. Can you say in Latin when they are (e.g. **natalis Carinae est die 2.° mensis Aprilis.**)?

Carina	Robertus	Helena	Clara	Claudius	Leo
die 2.° m. Aprilis	die 21.° m. Iunii	die 18.° m. Octobris	die 31.° m. Augusti	die 3.° m. Martii	die 7.° m. Septembris

*The Ancient Romans had a very different way of writing dates. Their system is explained on page 46.   39

Colors and numbers

Colors are adjectives (describing words). They have endings like **-us**, **-a**, **-um** and **-er**, **-a**, **-um**, which change according to the noun they are describing.

The colors

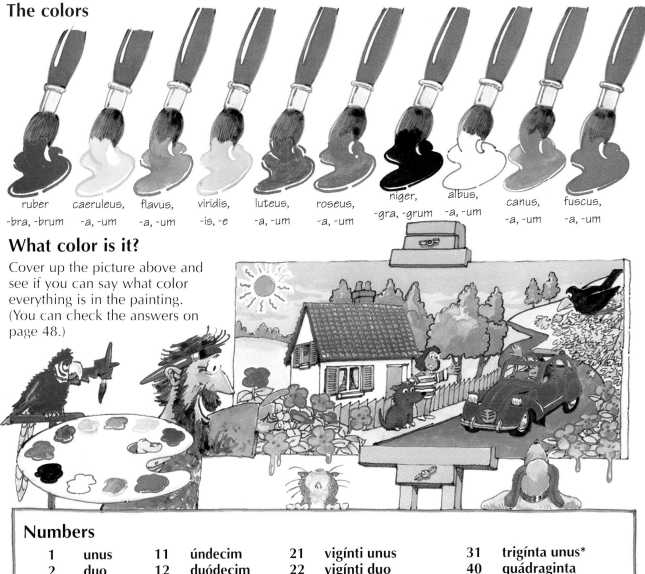

ruber	caeruleus,	flavus,	viridis,	luteus,	roseus,	niger,	albus,	canus,	fuscus,
-bra, -brum	-a, -um	-a, -um	-is, -e	-a, -um	-a, -um	-gra, -grum	-a, -um	-a, -um	-a, -um

What color is it?

Cover up the picture above and see if you can say what color everything is in the painting. (You can check the answers on page 48.)

Numbers

1	unus	11	úndecim	21	vigínti unus	31	trigínta unus*
2	duo	12	duódecim	22	vigínti duo	40	quádraginta
3	tres	13	trédecim	23	vigínti tres	50	quínquaginta
4	quáttuor	14	quattuórdecim	24	vigínti quattuor	60	séxaginta
5	quinque	15	quíndecim	25	vigínti quinque	70	séptuaginta
6	sex	16	sédecim	26	vigínti sex	80	óctoginta
7	septem	17	septéndecim	27	vigínti septem	90	nónaginta
8	octo	18	duodevigínti	28	duodetrigínta	100	centum
9	novem	19	undevigínti	29	undetrigínta	200	ducénti, -ae, -a
10	decem	20	vigínti	30	trigínta	1000	mille

*The rest of the numbers from 32 to 99 are formed in the same way; so you can figure them out for yourself. **duo-de**... means "two from..." and **un-de**... means "one from...."

Pronunciation and grammar

Nobody knows exactly what Latin sounded like when the Ancient Romans spoke it. Today Latin is pronounced slightly differently in different parts of the world. In English-speaking countries, the letters are usually pronounced as they are written. There are a few exceptions: **"c"** is always pronounced "k," **"v"** is pronounced "w," and **"i"** before a vowel at the beginning of a word is pronounced "y," For example, **iam** is pronounced "yam." In some books, this **"i"** is printed **"j,"** so it would be written **jam**, but is still pronounced "y."

Accentuation

In words of two syllables, such as **mensa**, the stress is put on the first syllable. In this book, words with more than two syllables have an accent mark over the syllable that needs to be stressed, like this: **música**. The stress is never on the last syllable. You should not write this accent, though. It is just there to help you pronounce the word.

Conjugation of verbs

The endings of Latin verbs change according to time (whether it is in the past, present or future) and person (I, you, we, etc.). This is called *conjugation*. The unchanging part of the verb is called the *stem*.

There are four regular types of verbs: those with an **"a"** stem (such as **ama-re**), those with an **"e"** stem (such as **habe-re**), those with a hard letter (or consonant) stem (such as **leg-ere**), and those with an **"i"** stem (such as **audi-re**).

Personal pronouns (I, you, we, etc) are not usual in Latin. You can tell which person it is by the verb ending. The endings are:

-o/m	I	**-mus**	we
-s	you	**-tis**	you (pl)
-t	he/she/it	**-nt**	they

Here are the four main types of verbs in the present tense.

1. The **"a"** stem

amare	to love
am-o	I love
ama-s	you love
ama-t	he/she/it loves
ama-mus	we love
ama-tis	you love
ama-nt	they love

2. The **"e"** stem

habere	to have
habe-o	I have
habe-s	you have
habe-t	he/she/it has
habe-mus	we have
habe-tis	you have
habe-nt	they have

3. The consonant stem

legere	to read
leg-o	I read
leg-i-s	you read
leg-i-t	he/she/it reads
leg-i-mus	we read
leg-i-tis	you read
leg-unt	they read

4. The **"i"** stem

audire	to hear
audi-o	I hear
audi-s	you hear
audi-t	he/she/it hears
audi-mus	we hear
audi-tis	you hear
audi-u-nt	they hear

The verb "to be"

esse	to be		
su-m	I am	**su-mus**	we are
e-s	you are	**es-tis**	you are
es-t	he/she/it is	**su-nt**	they are

Imperative forms

	"a" conj.	"e" conj.	"cons." conj.	"i" conj.
Sing.	**ama**	**habe**	**lege**	**audi**
Plur.	**amáte**	**habéte**	**légite**	**audíte**

41

More grammar

The future

The future tense of the 1st and 2nd conjugations is formed by adding **-bo**, **-bis**, **-bit** to the stem:

ama-b-o	I will love
ama-b-is	you will love
ama-b-it	he/she/it will love
ama-bi-mus	we will love
ama-bi-tis	you will love
ama-bu-nt	they will love
habe-b-o	I will have
habe-bi-s	you will have
habe-bi-t	he/she/it will have
habe-bi-mus	we will have
habe-bi-tis	you will have
habe-bu-nt	they will have

The future tense of 3rd and 4th conjugation verbs is formed by adding **-am**, **-es**, **-et** to the stem:

leg-a-m	I will read
leg-e-s	you will read
leg-e-t	he/she/it will read
leg-e-mus	we will read
leg-e-tis	you will read
leg-e-nt	they will read
audi-a-m	I will hear
audi-e-s	you will hear
audi-e-t	he/she/it will hear
audi-e-mus	we will hear
audi-e-tis	you will hear
audi-e-nt	they will hear

Declension and cases

The change in the endings of nouns, pronouns and adjectives is called *declension*. The different endings are called *cases*. Here are the names of the cases and a rough guide to their uses.

Nominative	For the subject of a sentence
Vocative	To speak to someone
Accusative	For the object of a sentence
Genitive	Used for "of"
Dative	Used for "to" or "for"
Ablative	Used for "by," "with," and "from"

The vocative has the same ending as the nominative, except with 2nd declension singular nouns ending in **-us**. The vocative ending for those is **-e**, e.g. **serve!** (slave!)

1st declension nouns

Example: **mensa** a table

	Singular	Plural
Nom.	**mens-a**	**mens-ae**
Acc.	**mens-am**	**mens-as**
Gen.	**mens-ae**	**mens-arum**
Dat.	**mens-ae**	**mens-is**
Abl.	**mens-a**	**mens-is**

2nd declension nouns

This declension includes nouns ending in **-us** and **-er** and neuter nouns ending in **-um**. Examples are **ann-us** (a year), **pu-er** (a boy) and **tect-um** (a roof).

	Singular	Plural
Nom.	**ann-us**	**ann-i**
Voc.	**ann-e**	**ann-i**
Acc.	**ann-um**	**ann-os**
Gen.	**ann-i**	**ann-orum**
Dat.	**ann-o**	**ann-is**
Abl.	**ann-o**	**ann-is**

Nouns ending in **-er** are different only in the nominative singular.

	Singular	Plural
Nom.	**tect-um**	**tect-a**
Acc.	**tect-um**	**tect-a**
Gen.	**tect-i**	**tect-orum**
Dat.	**tect-o**	**tect-is**
Abl.	**tect-o**	**tect-is**

In all neuter words, the ending of the accusative case (singular and plural) is the same as the ending of the nominative case.

3rd declension nouns

These nouns can be masculine, feminine or neuter. They have many different forms in the nominative singular.

Example: **canis, -is (m)** a dog

	Singular	Plural
Nom.	**canis**	**can-es**
Acc.	**can-em**	**can-es**
Gen.	**can-is**	**can-um**
Dat.	**can-i**	**can-ibus**
Acc.	**can-e**	**can-ibus**

Example: **aestas, -atis (f)** summer

	Singular	Plural
Nom.	**aestas**	**aestat-es**
Acc.	**aestat-em**	**aestat-es**
Gen.	**aestat-is**	**aestat-um**
Dat.	**aestat-i**	**aestat-ibus**
Abl.	**aestat-e**	**aestat-ibus**

1st and 2nd declension adjectives

These adjectives have the same feminine endings as nouns of the 1st declension. They have the same masculine and neuter endings as nouns of the 2nd declension.

Example: **bonus, -a, -um**, good

	Singular Masculine	Feminine	Neuter
Nom.	**bon-us**	**bon-a**	**bon-um**
Voc.	**bon-e**	**bon-a**	**bon-um**
Acc.	**bon-um**	**bon-am**	**bon-um**
Gen.	**bon-i**	**bon-ae**	**bon-i**
Dat.	**bon-o**	**bon-ae**	**bon-o**
Abl.	**bon-o**	**bon-a**	**bon-o**

	Plural Masculine	Feminine	Neuter
Nom.	**bon-i**	**bon-ae**	**bon-a**
Acc.	**bon-os**	**bon-as**	**bon-a**
Gen.	**bon-orum**	**bon-arum**	**bon-orum**
Dat.	**bon-is**	**bon-is**	**bon-is**
Abl.	**bon-is**	**bon-is**	**bon-is**

3rd declension adjectives

These adjectives all end in **-is** in the genitive singular. There are three groups. The plural is the same in all of them.

Group 1 (3 endings in the nom. sing.)

Example: **acer, -is**   sharp, fierce

	Singular Masculine	Feminine	Neuter
Nom.	**acer**	**acris**	**acre**
Acc.	**acrem**	**acrem**	**acre**
Gen.	**acris**	**acris**	**acris**
Dat.	**acri**	**acri**	**acri**
Abl.	**acri**	**acri**	**acri**

	Plural Masculine	Feminine	Neuter
Nom.	**acres**	**acres**	**acria**
Acc.	**acres**	**acres**	**acria**
Gen.	**acrium**	**acrium**	**acrium**
Dat.	**acribus**	**acribus**	**acribus**
Abl.	**acribus**	**acribus**	**acribus**

Group 2 (2 endings in nom. sing.)

Example: **fortis, -is**   brave, strong

	Singular Masculine	Feminine	Neuter
Nom.	**fortis**	**fortis**	**forte**
Acc.	**fortem**	**fortem**	**forte**
Gen.	**fortis**	**fortis**	**fortis**
Dat.	**forti**	**forti**	**forti**
Abl.	**forti**	**forti**	**forti**

Group 3 (1 ending in nom. sing.)

Example: **felix, -icis**   happy, lucky

	Singular Masculine	Feminine	Neuter
Nom.	**felix**	**felix**	**felix**
Acc.	**felicem**	**felicem**	**felix**
Gen.	**felicis**	**felicis**	**felicis**
Dat.	**felici**	**felici**	**felici**
Abl.	**felici**	**felici**	**felici**

Vocabulary

The nouns are shown with both their nominative and genitive endings. For example: **mensa, -ae** (f) table. **mensa** is nominative, **mensae** is genitive and (f) means the noun is feminine.

The other abbreviations are adv. (adverb), pl. (plural), pr. (present tense), irr. (irregular), acc. (accusative) and abl. (ablative).

Adjectives are shown in the nominative singular, with the masculine ending followed by the feminine and neuter ones. For example: **fuscus, -a, -um** brown.

Verbs are shown in the first person singular (I...), followed by the infinitive (to...). The declension number is also shown. For example: **amo/amare** 1 to love.

a sinistra parte	on the left side
ad + acc.	at, to
adeo/adire (irr.)	to go to
aestas, -atis (f)	summer
aliquid	something
amo/amare 1	to love
amica, -ae (f)	friend
amicus, -i (m)	friend
amita, -ae (f)	aunt (father's sister)
ananasa, -ae (f)	pineapple
Anglice	in English
annus, -i (m)	year
ante + acc.	in front of, before
Aprilis, -ilis (m)	April
aqua, -ae (f)	water
aranciata, -ae (f)	orange juice
arancium, -i (n)	an orange
arbor, -oris (f)	tree
argentaria, -ae (f)	bank
armarium, -i (n)	cupboard
athletica, -ae (f)	sport
audio/audire 4	to hear
Augustus, -i (m)	August
Austria, -ae (f)	Austria
aut	or
autocinetum, i (n)	auto, car
autoraeda, -ae (f)	auto, car
autumnus, -i (m)	autumn
avia, -ae (f)	grandmother
avis, is (f)	bird
avunculus, -i (m)	uncle (mother's brother)
avus, -i (m)	grandfather
balneum. -i (n)	bathroom
banana, -ae (f)	banana
bene	well, good!
bene tibi sapiat!	bon appetit!
bene valeo/valere 2	to be well
bonus, -a, -um	good
botulus, -i (m)	sausage
Britannia, -ae (f)	Britain
bubula assa, -ae, (f)	steak
butyrum, -i (n)	butter
cafea, -ae (f)	café, coffee
caminus, -i (m)	chimney
canicula, -ae (f)	puppy
canis, -is (m)	dog
cano, canere 3	to play
caseus, -i (m)	cheese
cena, -ae (f)	dinner
cenaculum (n)	dining room
chartula, -ae (f)	postcard
chiliogrammum, -i (n)	kilogram
cibaria,-orum (n.pl.)	food
cinema, -ae (f)	movies
citreum, -i (n)	lemon
clavarium, -i (n)	piano
cola, -ae (f)	cola
contra + acc.	across from, against
coquo/coquere 3	to cook
crassus, -a, -um	thick, fat
cricetus, -i (m)	hamster
cubiculum, -i (n)	bedroom
cum + abl.	with
curia, -ae (f)	city hall
do/dare 1	to give
decem	ten
December, -bris (m)	December
decimus, -a, -um	tenth
deinde	then
desidero/desiderare 1	to desire
deversorium, -i (n)	hotel
deverticulum juvenum (n)	youth hostel
dexter, -tra, -trum	right (-hand)
dextrorsum	to the right
dic mihi	tell me
dies, diei (m)	day
dies Iovis (m)	Thursday
dies Lunae (m)	Monday
dies Martis (m)	Tuesday
dies Mercurii (m)	Wednesday
dies Solis (m)	Sunday
dies Veneris (m)	Friday
dimidius -a, -um	half
discotheca (f)	disco
displicet mihi ...	I don't like ...
doleo/dolere 2 quod..	I am sorry that ...
domus, -us (f)	house
dormitum ire	to go to bed
duo, duae, duo	two
e, ex + abl.	from, out of
ecce!	here is, look!
ecclesia, -ae (f)	church
edo/edere 3	to eat
ego	I
eius	his, her, of him
emo/emere 3	to buy
eo/ire (irr.)	to go
eorum	their, of them
ergo	then, therefore
esurio/esurire 4	to be hungry
etiam	also, even
facio/facere 3	to do, to make
familia, -ae (f)	family, household
Februarius, -i (m)	February
feles, is (f)	cat
fenestra, -ae (f)	window
fere	almost, about
flavus, -a, -um	blond, yellow
flecte te	turn!
flos, floris (m)	flower
frater, -tris (m)	brother
fuscus, -a, -um	dark, brown
Germania, -ae (f)	Germany
Germanice	(in) German
glacies, -iei (f)	ice, an ice
gratias ago/agere 3	to thank
gracilis, -is, -e	thin
habeo/habere 2	to have
habito/habitare 1	to live in
Hammaburgensis, -is (m)	hamburger
Helvetia, -ae (f)	Switzerland
hic, haec, hoc	this
hiems, hiemis (f)	winter
Hispania, -ae (f)	Spain
hodie	today
holus, -eris (n)	vegetable
hora, -ae (f)	hour
Hungaria, -ae (f)	Hungary
hyalus, -i (m)	a glass
Ianuarius, -i (m)	January
ibi	there
ientaculum, -i (n)	breakfast
illic	there
in + acc.	into, onto
in + abl.	in, on
in directum	straight ahead
in propinquo	nearby
India, -ae (f)	India
instrumentum musicum, -i, (n)	musical instrument
inter + acc.	among, between
ire (pr. tense eo)	to go
is, ea, id	that
ita	so, thus
ita est	yes
Iulius, -i (m)	July
Iunius, -i (m)	June
lac, lactis (n)	milk
lactuca, -ae (f)	lettuce, salad
laniena, -ae (f)	butcher shop
larva, -ae (f)	ghost
Latine	(in) Latin
lego/legere 3	to read
libra, -ae (f)	a pound (weight)
librarium, -i (n)	bookcase
limonata, -ae (f)	lemonade
Londini	in London
longinquus, -a, -um	distant, far away
loquor/loqui 3 dep.	to talk

ludo/ludere 3	to play (a game)
Lutetiae	in Paris
magnus, -a, um	large, big
Maius, -i (m)	May
malum, -i (n)	apple
mane (adv. & noun)	(in the) morning
mare, maris (n)	sea
Martius, -i (m)	March
mater, -tris (f)	mother
matertera, -ae (f)	aunt (mother's sister)
maxime	very much, most
media nox, mediae noctis (f)	midnight
medianum, -i (n)	living room
mensa, -ae (f)	table
mensis, -is (m)	month
meridies, -iei (m)	noon
meus, -a, -um	my
mihi (dat. of ego)	to me, for me
mihi est/sunt...	I have ...
mihi placet...	I like ...
minime	not at all, least
minuta, -ae (f)	minute
musica, -orum (n.pl)	music
nam	for
natalis, -is (m)	birthday
nato/natare 1	to swim
natus, -a, -um	born (old)
-ne	(asks a question)
neque ... neque	neither ... nor
nidus, -i (m)	nest
nihil laboris est	it's no trouble
nolo/nolle (irr.)	I do not want
nomen, -inis (n)	name
non	not
nonus, -a, -um	ninth
novem	nine
November, -bris (m)	November
octavus, -a, -um	eighth
officium postale (n)	Post Office
omnia, -ium (n. pl)	everything
optime	very good, excellent
oryza, -ae (f)	rice
ovum, -i (n)	egg
paene	almost, nearly
palatium, -i (n)	palace
panicellus, -i (m)	roll, bun
panis, -is (m)	bread
parentes, -ium (m)	parents
pars, partis (f)	part
parvus, -a, -um	small, little
pasta vermiculata -ae, -ae (f)	spaghetti
pater, -tris (m)	father
patruus, -i (m)	uncle (father's brother)
paulum (adv.)	a little
pedibus	on foot, walking
pedifollis, -is (m)	football
pediludium -i (n)	football
perna, -ae (f)	ham
persicum, -i (n)	peach
pessime (adv.)	very bad, terrible
phamacopola, -ae (f)	pharmacy
pingo/pingere 3	to paint
piscina, -ae (f)	swimming pool
pitta, -ae (f)	pizza
placenta, -ae (f)	cake
planta, -ae (f)	plant
plasso/plassare 1	to make models
poma terrestria assa (n.pl)	french fries
pomum, -i (n)	fruit
porta, -ae (f)	door, gate
possum/posse (irr.)	to be able
post + acc.	behind, after
potus socolatae (m)	chocolate drink
praefectura (-ae commeatus (f)	travel information bureau
praefero/-ferre (irr.)	to prefer
prandium, -i (n)	lunch
primus, -a, -um	first
pistrina, -ae (f)	bakery
prope + acc.	near
proximus, -a, -um	next, nearest
puella, -ae (f)	girl
puer, -i (m)	boy
qua via?	by what road? how?
quadrans, -ntis (m)	a quarter
quaero/quaerere 3	to look for, ask
quaeso	please
quando?	when?
quanti constat/ constant ...?	how much does...cost?
quartus, -a, -um	fourth
quattuor	four
-que	and
qui dies hodie est?	what day is it today?
quid?	what?
quid aliud?	what else?
quinque	five
quintus, -a, -um	fifth
quis?	who?
quod nomen?	what name?
quoque	also
quot?	how many?
quota hora est?	what time is it?
ratio, -ionis (f)	check, bill
reperio/reperire 4	to find
requiro/requirere 3	to want
Romae	in Rome
rosa, -ae (f)	rose
ruri	in the country
saeptum, -i (n)	fence
salto/saltare 1	to dance
salve!	hello!
sapio/sapere 3	to taste
sapitne bene?	does it taste good?
satis (adv.)	enough
schola, -ae (f)	school
scio/scire 4	to know (how to...)
scriblita, -ae (f)	a tart
secundus, -a, -um	second
sed	but
sella, -ae (f)	armchair
septem	seven
September, -bris (m)	September
septimus, -a, -um	seventh
sex	six
sextus, -a, -um	sixth
sinister, -tra, -trum	left
sol, -is (m)	sun
soror, -oris (f)	sister
specto/spectare 1	to look at, gaze at
sponda, -ae (f)	sofa
stabulum autocinetum (n)	garage
statio ferriviaria (f)	railroad station
sub + abl.	under
sum/esse (irr.)	to be
supermercatus, -us (m)	supermarket
surgo/surgere 3	to rise
taberna, -ae (f)	shop, tavern
taberna alimentaria (f)	grocery store
tabulatum, -i (n)	story, floor
tapete, -is (n)	carpet
tectum, -i (n)	roof
telephonum, -i (n)	telephone
televisorium, -i (n)	television
tener, -era, -erum	gentle
teniludium, -i (n)	tennis
tertius, -a, -um	third
texo/texere 3	to weave, knit
thea, -ae (f)	tea
tibi (dat. of tu)	to you, for you
tibi est/sunt...	you have ...
tomata, -ae (f)	tomato
tres, tres, tria	three
tu (acc. = te)	you (singular)
tum	then
tuus, -a, -um	your
ubi?	where?
unde?	where from?
unus, -a, -um	one
urbis, urbis (f)	city
usque ad diem crastinum	until tomorrow
ut	how
uva, -ae (f)	grape
valde	very much
vale!	goodbye!
valeo/valere 3	to be well
vasculum, -i (n)	vase
vehere!	drive!
velim	I would like
velum, -i (n)	curtain, sail
venio/venire 4	to come
ver, -is (n)	spring
vesperi	in the evening
vestibulum, -i (n)	entrance hall
veterrimus, -a, -um	very old, oldest
via, -ae (f)	road, street
vicesmus, -a, -um	twentieth
viginti	twenty
violina, -ae (f)	violin
volo/velle (irr.)	to want
visne?	do you want?

Numbers, dates, and time

How the Romans told time

The Romans divided the daylight, from sunrise to sunset, into twelve equal hours. These hours varied in length as the days became longer or shorter, depending on the time of year. **hora prima** always started at sunrise, and **hora septima** always started at noon. The night was divided into four equal **vigiliae** (meaning "watches"). **vigilia prima** was from sunset to approximately 9 p.m. **vigilia tertia** always started at midnight. The Romans only had water clocks and sun dials to help them tell the time, and these were not very convenient.

Roman Numbers

The signs the Romans used for numbers were **I** (one), **V** (five), **X** (ten), **L** (50), **C** (100), **D** (500), **M** (1000).

In most cases, you can identify the other numbers by adding the signs together. This works for signs of equal value next to each other. For example, **III** = 3 and **CCC** = 300. It also works if the sign of a larger value is followed by a smaller one. For example, **VIII** = 8, **XXVII** = 27, **LXI** = 61, and **CCLVII** = 257.

But if a sign is followed by one of a larger value, the first sign is subtracted from the second, larger one. For example, **IV**= 4, (**I** is subtracted from **V**), **IX** = 9, **XLIV** = 44, **XC** = 90, **CM** = 900, **MCM** = 1900, **MCMXCVIII** = 1998.

Can you figure out what these numbers are: **XXXIX, CCXLVII, MLXVI, MDCCXXIV, MMMDCCLXXIX**?

How would you write these numbers in Roman numerals: 17, 59, 385, 1234, 4321?

Roman dates

The names of the different months of the year come from the names the Romans used. After the time of Julius Caesar, the Roman months were the same as ours, except that they had no leap year, and no names for days and weeks. There were three fixed times in each month. The first day of the month was always called the **Kalends**. For most months of the year, the fifth day was called the **Nones** and the thirteenth day was called the **Ides**. But in March, May, July and October, the **Nones** and **Ides** were the seventh and fifteenth days.

The Romans described the date in relation to the next fixed point. So, for example, January 31st was "the day before the Kalends of February." They wrote this as **pridie KAL.FEB.**

The Romans included the days on which they started and finished counting. So January 30th was "three days before the Kalends of February," or "the third day before the Kalends of February" : **antediem tertium KAL. FEB.** This was usually abbreviated to **a.d.III KAL. FEB.**

Here are a few more examples:

February 1st was **KAL. FEB.** February 2nd was **a.d.IV NON. FEB** (four days before the Nones). February 4th was **pridie NON. FEB.** February 5th was **NON. FEB.** February 6th was **a.d.VIII ID. FEB.**

See if you can translate these modern dates into Roman ones: March 15, April 3, June 10, July 24, October 6, November 1. The answers are at the bottom of the page. (Note: **Ides** were abbreviated to **ID**.)

Answers:

Roman numbers: 39, 247, 1066, 1724, 3779: XVII, LIX, CCCLXXXV, MCCXXXIV, MMMMCCCXXI.

Roman dates: **ID. MAR.; a.d.III NON. APR.; a.d.IV ID JUN.; a.d.IX KAL. AUG.; pridie NON. OCT.; KAL. NOV.**

Who is saying what?

"esurio!"
"bene tibi sapiat."
"sume aliquid, quaeso!"
"potesne mihi dare hyalum?"
"visne etiam poma terrestria assa?"
"volo. amo pomo terrestria assa."
"nolo. satis est."
"optime sapit."

What are they doing?

A coquit B natat C saltant D violina canit
E pingit

Questions and answers

quid facis?	coquo.
quid facis?	nato.
quid facitis?	saltamus.
quid facis?	violina cano.
quid facis?	pingo.

Marcus's day

1B, 2E, 3F, 4A, 5H, 6G, 7D, 8C.

What time is it?

A quinque minutis post tertiam horam.
B quinque minutis post undecimam horam.
C octo minutis ante nonam horam.
D quadrante ante quartam horam.
E viginti quinque minutis post tertiam horam.
F septima hora et dimidia.
G tertia hora.
H quarta hora.
I nona hora.
J prima hora et dimidia.
K quinque minutis post septimam horam.
L decima hora et dimidia.
M sexta hora.
N viginti quinque minutis ante quartam horam.
O septem minutis ante secundam horam.

Your diary for the week

vesperi saltabo cum Tito.
die Lunae, Mercurii, Solis teniludio ludo.
die Martis secunda hora clavario cano.

In Messina

qua via ad forum venio/adibo? da mihi veniam, estne cafea in propinquo? cape tertiam viam a dextra, deinde vehere semper in directum. cape tertiam viam a sinistra, deinde vehere semper in directum.

To the school.

Buying fruit

requiro quattuor citrea, unam libram bananarum et unam ananasam. quattuor citrea constant sexaginta sestertiis, una libra bananarum constat quinquaginta octo sestertiis, et una ananasa constat centum decem sestertiis. omnia constant ducentis quinquaginta sestertiis. una ananasa. una libra persicarum. tria arancia constant sexaginta sex sestertiis. una libra malorum constat quinquaginta quinque sestertiis.

When are their birthdays?

natalis Roberti est die vicesmo primo m. Iunii.
natalis Helenae est die duodevicesmo m. Octobris.
natalis Clarae est die tricesimo primo m. Augusti.
natalis Claudii est die tertio m. Martii.
natalis Leonis est die septimo m. Septembris.

What color is it?

via cana est. sol flavus est. tectum luteum est. caelum caeruleum est. flores rosei sunt. canis fuscus est. avis nigra est. autocinetum rubrum est. arbores virides sunt. domus alba est.

Answers to puzzles

Page 7

What are their names?

nomen eius Petrus est.
nomen eius Claudia est.
nomina eorum Paulus et Petrus sunt.
nomen meum est...

Who is who?

Lucius is speaking to Quintus.
Cornelia is speaking to Beata.
Lucius is swimming, bottom right, with a
    green bathing-cap.
Quintus is talking to him.
Carolus is reading the paper.
The man saying "good-bye" to Carolus.

Can you remember?

quod nomen tibi est?
nomen meum est ...
haec amica mea est. nomen eius Beata est.
hic amicus meus est. nomen eius Gaius est.

Page 9

Can you remember?

hic flos est. haec feles est.
haec arbor est. hic nidus est.
haec avis est. haec domus est.
hic sol est. haec fenestra est.
hoc autocinetum est. hic canis est.

Page 11

Who comes from where?

Franciscus comes from Austria.
Arius and Indira.
Lolita is Spanish.
Janus lives in Budapest (Hungary).
Yes, Angus comes from Scotland.
Marie and Pierre come from France.
Budapest is in Hungary.

Can you remember?

unde venis.   venio e/ex...
scio loqui Latine.   scisne loqui Latine?

Page 13

How old are they?

Afer is 13.   Livia is 11.
Diana and Sylvia are 15.   Lucius is 9.
Titus is 12.   Aemilia is 5.

Brothers and sisters

A = Diana et Sylvia B = Lucius C = Afer
D = Titus E = Livia

Page 17

Where is everyone?

avus in cenaculo est.
Quintus in coquina est.
Petrus in balneo est.
mater in cubiculo est.

avia in mediano est.
larva in cubiculo Isabellae est.
Isabella in summo tabulato est.
Petrus in balneo est.

Can you remember?

ego in urbe habito, tu ruri. cubiculum in
summo tabulato est. avia in insula habitat.
Quintus est in balneo. habitamus in domo.

Page 19

Where are the animals hiding?

cricetus in vasculo est.
feles parva ad televisorium est.
canicula in armario est.
psittacus in librario est.
serpens sub sponda est.
testudo prope telephonum est.

Page 21

Who likes what

Henricus caseum amat.
Nemo pernam amat.
avus uvas praefert.
amo/non amo…

1996 Printing

This edition first published in 1995 by Passport Books, A Division of NTC Publishing Group, 4255 W. Touhy Avenue, Lincolnwood (Chicago), Illinois 60646-1975 USA. © 1995 NTC Publishing Group and Usborne Publishing Ltd.

Printed in Great Britain.